BUILDING CITIES FROM SCRATCH

Building Cities from Scratch:
America's Long History of Urban Experimentation

by Steven Greenhut

September 2024

ISBN: 978-1-934276-56-3

Pacific Research Institute
P.O. Box 60485
Pasadena, CA 91116

www.pacificresearch.org

Nothing contained in this report is to be construed as necessarily reflecting the views of the Pacific Research Institute or as an attempt to thwart or aid the passage of any legislation. The views expressed remain solely the author. They are not endorsed by any of the author's past or present affiliations.

BUILDING CITIES FROM SCRATCH
AMERICA'S LONG HISTORY OF
URBAN EXPERIMENTATION

By Steven Greenhut

VOLUME SIX

PRI PACIFIC
RESEARCH
INSTITUTE

New City Plan Falters, But Sparks Needed Debate

SOME OF THE MOST contentious public-policy issues that dominate the public's attention focus understandably on what architects and planners call our "built environment" – the neighborhoods, offices, shopping centers, infrastructure and parks that are the backdrops for our day-to-day existence. Consider the big problems in California and the West: high housing prices, sprawling homeless encampments, traffic congestion and street crime.[1] These all are "built environment" issues, even though policymakers typically address them in a piecemeal fashion.

Some activists do indeed look at such matters from a broader perspective. YIMBYs (Yes In My Back Yarders) and other urbanists have had much recent legislative success (particularly in California, Oregon and Washington) pushing an agenda – some of it good, some of it less so – that's driven by an overarching vision of how cities and suburbs should be designed. It doesn't take much digging to understand their perspective. They dislike car-dependent suburbs and want most of us to live in densely packed neighborhoods and get around by transit or bicycle.[2]

Advocates for this worldview, which dominates planning agencies and academic departments, often use the language of "choice" and "markets" – but their ideas are mostly driven by government edict and subsidy. They rightly want to reduce government restrictions on housing construction, but only to the degree that it encourages the particular type of housing they prefer (high-density, transit-oriented apartments and condos). They want Americans to have the choice to live in denser settings, but push back when consumers choose single-family suburban housing. When one points out their hypocrisy, they argue that climate change makes that choice unsustainable.[3]

On the other side, we find NIMBYs (Not In My Back Yarders), who act as if their current suburban-style living arrangements are enshrined in the Constitution – or the result of free markets rather than partly the creation of government zoning and land-use rules.[4] The YIMBYs tend to be utopian, in that they want to remake the entire built environment in their vision (albeit an old vision that sprouted in the pre-automobile era). By contrast, the NIMBYs are devoted to freezing our communities in place, by using government to restrict the kind of change the market may be demanding.

That's largely where the housing debate has been – a fight between those who push incremental zoning reforms to encourage higher densities and those who defend existing zoning to maintain the "character" of their neighborhoods. Then we see bitter debates about how to house the homeless, many of whom have turned public spaces into tent cities. And the related transportation battles are heated, also. Urbanists demand new public spending on bus and rail systems, even as the public largely votes with their feet (or their gas pedals). Few transit systems have recovered not only from hemorrhaging COVID-19 ridership, but from years of falling ridership.[5]

But sometimes a big proposal can help break us out of a public-policy rut. Such is the case with a contentious plan from some Bay Area venture capitalists to build an entirely new city in an exurban and rural area around 55 miles east of San Francisco and 45 miles southwest of Sacramento, called the East Solano Plan. Instead of fighting over small-scale land-use changes that allow more select types of housing around the margins, its backers proposed building an entire city from scratch on 17,500 acres. Flannery Associates and its California Forever project envisioned 50,000 new residents following initial completion of the first phase, with as many as 400,000 residents "many decades" into the future.[6]

> *But sometimes a big proposal can help break us out of a public-policy rut.*

In a surprising move, the plan's leaders in late July 2024 pulled their land-use proposal from the November ballot after spending 10 months promoting it. A negative report from the county and poor polling data apparently convinced California Forever to delay the proposal, work with the county on an Environmental Impact Report and bring it back in 2026.[7] Although this matter – the source of much debate in Northern California – has been delayed, the plan sparked a much-needed debate about the importance of building new cities and planned communities as California faces a continuing housing crisis. It's useful to review the plan and why it failed to move forward as the state looks at ways to boost housing production.

Unlike many proposed new suburban communities, which focus mainly on houses with some tangential retail, religious and commercial projects, California Forever planned to build a more traditional city complete with a downtown and walkable communities. It utilized all the New Urbanist buzzwords. The group had to gather signatures to place before voters a measure to re-jigger the county's master plan (necessary because of the Orderly Growth Initiative that voters overwhelmingly approved in 1984 and then was extended in 1994 and 2008).[8] It made the following promise:

> Create homes in safe, walkable neighborhoods, wherein for-sale and for-rent homes at different price points are integrated in the same neighborhoods, and wherein all residents and workers can not only drive but also have the option to walk, bike, or take transit to work, schools, stores, restaurants, parks and places of worship, and wherein the community is expressly designed to accommodate the needs of children, families and seniors.[9]

The project grabbed public attention – across the country, and not just in Northern California – after *The New York Times* reported in August 2023 that, "A mysterious company has spent $800 million in an effort to buy thousands of acres of San Francisco Bay Area land. The people behind the deals are said to be a who's who of the tech industry."[10] The secretive land acquisition – and aggressive tactics, as the company sued local ranchers for alleged price fixing – echoed Walt Disney's infamous, secretive acquisition of 30,000 acres of central Florida swampland to build Disney World.[11] In fact, local residents and officials were largely unaware of the project until the *Times* article.

The *Times* referred to an email in 2017 to potential investors from billionaire Michael Moritz that envisioned a "bustling metropolis that, according to the pitch, could generate thousands of jobs and be as walkable as Paris or the West Village in New York. He painted a kind of urban blank slate where everything from design to construction methods and new forms of governance could be re-thought."[12] That possible rethinking is what caught my attention – and the interest of many theorists who are interested in the future of urban planning. Given all the ongoing urban crises, the idea of an urban blank slate is appealing and intriguing.

On its website,[13] California Forever goes beyond the usual, albeit solid arguments for new developments (the need for housing that locals can afford, the creation of new job centers to reduce commuting, the blah-blah-blah "green" approaches the developers have embraced, etc.). Given the sophistication of its backers, it's not surprising that the proposal delved deeply into complex urban-planning concepts in making the "urbanist case" for a new city. Because of California's progressive tilt, the group's public-relations efforts seem mindful of the type of people they need to win over. Some of its hired guns have extensive experience in the state's Democratic politics.

"All cities were once 'new' cities," California Forever explains. "In a comparatively young country like America, many can still remember the founding of formerly new cities that are now sizable."[14] It points to British urban planner Ebenezer Howard's late 19th-century Garden Cities movement, which tried to create small satellite cities, separated by greenbelts, as a way to help people escape the filth, congestion and poverty of London and other British industrial cities.

Then California Forever refers to the New Urbanist movement, which sprung up in the 1990s as a retort to spreading suburbanization. That movement, which has since been eclipsed by a more rigid and statist form of urbanism, was a design ideal that promoted walkability and traditional urban values. But California Forever insists that it's not trying to just build another New Urbanist community such as Seaside, Fla., the stylish beachside community that served as a backdrop to the dystopian movie, "The Truman Show." In its view, those have been too small. (And, I'd add that they mainly are enclaves for the wealthy and have an overly manicured quality about them.) Instead, the Solano project wanted to implement those concepts on a much larger scale and within a "real" city that's home to diverse income groups. This is from California Forever's website:[15]

> We are attempting something that has not been done in a century – to create a new community that has density, mixed use, public life and scale. The scale matters not just because it's a bigger contribution to housing needs, but because it means we can get to critical mass to support services and jobs, so it does not end up as a "bedroom community." …. At the same time, the scale of the new community means that we have to solve problems of bigger places. … The inspiration for the California Forever approach to city planning is not so much New Urbanism as it is the early plans of the 19th-century American cities.

The audaciousness of the plan was its strength and, ultimately, its downfall. Leave it to Bay Area venture capitalists to not just propose a massive new development with some New Urbanist "farkles" – but to insist that they are reimagining the entire urban-planning process. Typical of that world, their proposal attempted something that hasn't been done before (or at least not in a century). It planned to create something that competes not only with nearby bedroom communities, but with the most significant urban designs in American history, namely New York City's and San Francisco's. As I explain later, the concept isn't particularly new. Forward-looking developers built a variety of new, walkable cities in the 1960s and 1970s. Such ideas date to the 1800s.

As a journalist, I'm naturally jaded by grandiose promises. When I covered the origination of the Great Park in Orange County, Calif., in the early 2000s, its supporters promised that it would rival Golden Gate Park in San Francisco or Central Park in Manhattan. Being somewhat cynical, I realized that it was mainly an attempt to lure voters into supporting an initiative that promised something other than the county's proposed (but now-scuttled) international airport – and that the economics of it would never justify the promises. I dubbed it the Great *Pork*,[16] a project that would consume mass amounts of public pork-barrel funding. Twenty two years later, it's basically as predicted – a financial sinkhole, albeit with some private housing and commercial developments and a few ordinary park amenities (plus a silly orange hot-air balloon ride) scattered around the massive site. The privately built portions (sold off to developers) of the site have done predictably well, but the public park portions are underwhelming.

That was mainly a government-driven concept. The Solano city idea was driven by private investors with a track record of building enterprises (although not new cities). That makes it a much more enticing and doable idea. Even if it ultimately became little more than a collection of new housing developments and office parks (with a few sterile "downtown" areas not unlike those built in affluent suburbs such as El Dorado Hills, Calif., and Brea, Calif.),[17] and managed along the lines of standard unincorporated county governance, it's still a worthwhile thought experiment. California is desperate for new housing. Still, the possibilities it raises are enticing as the state struggles with all the endemic urban-governance problems.

Before the latest problems, the project ran into predictable obstacles. Because of the previously mentioned Solano County urban-growth initiatives, California Forever had to win over local officials and the public. It had assembled a large team of supporters and has been holding events in affected cities. As is typical with any major development proposal, local critics have shown up and meetings have at times become emotional. NIMBY groups have of course fought the measure, but these Bay Area bigwigs have given off the arrogant air often associated with that crowd.

Their lawsuit against local ranchers seemed almost designed to alienate rural populations.[18] They've previously had to adjust their plan to accommodate concerns from nearby Travis Air Force Base.[19]

But it's no surprise that visionaries might not do politics particularly well. As CBS News reported in March, "The Solano County government put out an alert warning voters that it had, 'received multiple reports of voters being misinformed by circulators collecting signatures either with incorrect information or for a petition to stop the East Solano Homes, Jobs and Clean Energy Initiative,' which is also known as the California Forever campaign."[20] The Sierra Club and other anti-growth environmental groups issued overheated opposition statements related to land conservation, as expected.[21]

The region's members of Congress adamantly opposed the project. U.S. Reps. John Garamendi, D-Fairfield, and Mike Thompson, D-Napa, promote fears about privatization.[22] At a February 2024 press conference, Garamendi expressed concern about "the inability of the county government to control what goes on in this

400,000-person city. No city council, no local government to be set up at all." Said Thompson: "This isn't a proposal for a city, this is a proposal for a development and it would be the developers … calling the shots in their development."[23] Such concerns seemed overblown. The backers didn't delve into governance issues, but suggested the city might be governed by the county, which is normal for new developments that are not incorporated as cities. It would be great for a new city to privatize services or rethink the way such services are provided. The nation's last major experiment in such privatization took place in Sandy Springs, Ga., which privatized many public services outside policing but eventually brought most of them back in house.[24] I suspect that California Forever downplayed more innovative possibilities as a means to reduce opposition to the land-use initiative.

The county report is what likely scuttled the project. The biggest problem was the potential infrastructure cost, according to the county: "The financial feasibility of the project is questionable given high projected infrastructure costs of $6.4 billion for Phase 1 to $49.1 billion at buildout, without identified funding sources. Ongoing maintenance of infrastructure would come at a cost to Solano County and all residents, including those outside the new community. The largest costs follow."[25] The project's backers clearly need to do a better job detailing exactly how these significant costs – even if inflated by county planners – would be handled.

In my role at the Free Cities Center and as a newspaper columnist, I've reached out multiple times to California Forever spokespeople, consultants and investors to discuss some of these issues in depth, but my repeated requests over several months have been ignored even though I've published favorable pieces about the proposal. That confirms my fears that the group hasn't learned how to build coalitions or isn't interested in doing so. In fact, the *Times* article is what seemed to push California Forever to finally begin engaging with the public.

In a Free Cities Center video, I interview Nick McConnell, a reporter with the *Vacaville Reporter* who has covered the issue closely throughout Solano County. Local residents were "frustrated that they didn't come out and say 'this is what we're doing," he noted, in reference to the five-year effort to secretly buy parcels. It led to much unnecessary public frustration. In reference to California Forever's lawsuit against some ranch owners, alleging price fixing, one resident spoke at the Rio Vista town hall and said, "neighbors don't sue neighbors," McConnell added.[26] That action loomed over the discussions given the importance of farming in the region.

One needn't like the developers' reluctance to talk or their overall PR approach to see the value in what they were planning. The state's current urban policies aren't working. It's time for something to shake up the status quo. There's nothing like building a city from scratch to open up new possibilities and to provide needed housing supply. McConnell adds that part of California Forever's pitch is to "young people priced out of the area and to those who love those people. … This is a place your kids can live."[27] That is a good argument.

The debate clearly sharpens the lines between those who want the rural/exurban region to remain as it has been – and those who are concerned about a housing-affordability crisis that is making it tough for younger generations to build their own lives. Even with the project delayed, this important discussion needs to continue.

The Hypocrisy of the 'Just Build Housing' YIMBYs

CALIFORNIA FOREVER'S STATEMENT THAT "all cities were once new cities" is worth contemplating. The urban-planning profession is dominated by people who seem to have forgotten that obvious point, as they idealize existing cities and snarl at the idea of new construction in undeveloped areas. Indeed, the modern urbanist movement – and many Western states' official policies – are driven by the requirement that most new construction should take place within the existing urban footprint.[28]

That's one reason California's housing affordability problem has blossomed into a crisis. It's more expensive to build within that footprint – and these policies have stopped many planned proposals elsewhere. Some major proposals for master-planned communities and new cities have been stymied for decades, as environmentalists file CEQA (California Environmental Quality Act) and other lawsuits.[29] And despite concerns about urban sprawl, Western states in particular have vast amounts of open landscape. I just drove from the Canadian border near Vancouver, B.C., to Sacramento – and the endless open spaces belie the overcrowding myth. Oregon has fewer than 40 people per square mile. California, with its 39-million population, has only 258 people per square mile – far lower than the nations that urbanists compare us to as justification for, say, their California high-speed rail project.

New Urbanism started as an urban-design concept. By contrast, Smart Growth is the planning arm of the urbanist movement, which promotes various limits and growth-stifling policies such as Portland-style urban-growth boundaries. As *Smart Growth Online* explains,[30] this philosophy "directs development towards existing communities already served by infrastructure, seeking to utilize the resources that existing neighborhoods offer, and conserve open space and irreplaceable natural resources on the urban fringe. … The ease of greenfield development remains an obstacle to encouraging more development in existing neighborhoods. Development on the fringe remains attractive to developers for its ease of access and construction, lower land costs, and potential for developers to assemble larger parcels."

Housing affordability is a stated concern of urbanists, so it's odd for them to insist that building in the highest-priced regions, on the trickiest parcels in the highest-taxed locales with the costliest infrastructure limitations and union-dominated construction trades is the way to build enough housing to bring down prices for would-be buyers. When the Free Cities Center interviewed a Sacramento official about the city's efforts to encourage housing along the R Street Corridor, he noted that it's too costly to build new projects or remodel old ones in the urban core without subsidies.[31] Urbanist opposition to "greenfield" development suggests that their goal isn't primarily to promote housing construction but to de-suburbanize our society.

That outlook offers a conundrum for supporters of new cities. California Forever made the "urbanist case" for its project, arguing that the project "offers a model for how to create new communities that provide the benefits of dense, walkable life to more people. If the new community is ever built, it will become a demonstration of some sensible approaches to city planning that can be deployed to other cities, both old and new." A few urbanists and YIMBYs were supportive, but many activists in that movement have actively opposed it. Others have remained oddly quiet – odd because urbanists love to talk about every tiny building proposal that takes place. Read their posts on X and you're unlikely to find a bigger group of neighborhood busybodies. They comment on everything, from the facades of new buildings to the grittiest detail of new bike lanes to the brightness of streetlights to the size of parking spaces. To its credit, the state's main YIMBY group, California YIMBY, did ultimately issue a statement of support in June 2024.[32]

The YIMBY mantra has been "just build housing,"[33] but the movement's critics (this writer included) have long noted that the saying needs an asterisk after it: *Only high-density housing in existing cities of the type and style that we like applies here.* This project, although delayed, shines a light on their inconsistencies, as California Forever most definitely would have built more housing and provided walkable communities. It promised front porches and a vibrant downtown. But it would have done so on open ranchland miles from existing urban areas. Most people who might live there almost certainly would buy dreaded cars.

I've also talked with NIMBY critics of the plan,[34] who raise questions about whether the project will be able to lure enough businesses, whether there's sufficient infrastructure to support the project and whether people will really want to live that far from existing job centers. Some complain about water scarcity, even though the project is on the edge of the California Delta, the West Coast's largest estuary and the most water-rich site in California.

Yes, California policymakers need to do a better job building infrastructure and improving the state's water and energy systems, but we shouldn't deny new housing construction for that reason. For one thing, the state's population isn't even growing – the likely residents of the new city already live here and already are using resources. As an aside, environmentalists have long opposed resource and infrastructure improvements as de facto growth controls. Yet developers are capable of addressing supply and demand issues. They are capable of building and funding infrastructure to serve a new project. They actually are required to do so. They aren't going to invest their own money into a project if they haven't done the calculations. Projects evolve and markets work. I suspect these naysayers are just concocting excuses not to support the plan. These Luddite arguments shouldn't dissuade us.

Regarding the YIMBYs, the *San Francisco Chronicle* addressed[35] their mixed reactions and some of their hypocrisy. The newspaper found one YIMBY movement founder, Sonja Trauss, who spoke favorably about it: "I'm excited about it – more is more, and we need housing. I'm from Philadelphia, so it's not unprecedented or weird to me that rich people would try to found a city. (Philadelphia founder) William Penn was a rich guy. He got a land grant and built a city on a grid. He created something innovative and beautiful."

Kudos to her, but others quoted from that movement were critical. Another prominent YIMBY called it "sprawl 2.0." The newspaper noted that, "Other YIMBYs argued that the amount of money and attention going into the California Forever project will lessen the chances that dense infill housing will be added in Solano County cities like Fairfield, which has been desperately and unsuccessfully looking to attract multifamily developers to its downtown – which is the county seat and boasts a train station, large urban park, courthouses and administrative buildings."[36]

It's a weird argument from advocates of more housing that the government should stop a project that promises to house tens of thousands of people because, well, building new stuff out there will stop people from building stuff over here, where we think it ought to go. Nothing – beyond the usual building fees and regulations – is stopping YIMBYs from building infill

Yes, California policymakers need to do a better job building infrastructure and improving the state's water and energy systems, but we shouldn't deny new housing construction for that reason.

housing in downtown Fairfield, Suisun City or Vacaville. Both types of projects are possible at the same time, especially given ongoing housing supply problems in Northern California.

The group, Solano Together, reflects the main organized opposition to the project. It states on its website that its goal is "to support development and infrastructure investment in existing cities to preserve vital farm and ranch lands and prevent harmful sprawl development."[37] It also supports "public and private efforts to address the state and regional housing crises through development of affordable and market-rate housing in existing communities that are legally required to accommodate over 10,000 housing units in the next decade alone."[38]

That reinforces my long-held view that many YIMBYs and NIMBYs are often similar in their willingness to use government to limit housing construction. Their only real difference is NIMBYs don't want that construction within their existing communities and YIMBYs do. Neither side advocates for more overall housing construction wherever the market determines it ought to go.

The Shameful Mismanagement of Our Current Big Cities

CURRENT URBAN MISMANAGEMENT IS a key reason building new cities is a good idea. I suspect that many urbanists don't like new cities because new cities pose a challenge via competition to existing ones. And those existing ones are often poorly run. I've always found it ironic that urbanists insist that new development be focused within existing big cities while ignoring the day-to-day concerns of the potential residents: parks overrun by open-air drug markets and tent cities, poor-performing public schools, rising crime, dirty transit systems, high taxes and bureaucracy run amok.[39]

Maybe there are legitimate reasons that most Americans don't want to abandon their relatively safe and well-run suburbs for this promised urban bliss. My daughter is a diehard San Franciscan who lives in a fairly nice neighborhood. Even she is thinking of leaving for the suburbs given the crime, trash, open drug dealing and constant vehicle break-ins on her block. Urbanists don't offer many solutions to those real problems. Their dismissal of serious resident concerns is elitist. Consider, also, that San Francisco as well as Seattle and other major Western big cities are largely childless cities.[40] It's too hard to raise a family there given these challenges and the high cost of living.

Bigger cities have particularly liberal voting populations, which tend to support politicians who advocate higher taxes, rent controls, limits on school choice and other policies that erode the quality of life for average residents. San Francisco's voters have pushed back recently. In the March 2024 primary, they passed measures that expanded police powers, allowed developers more flexibility and required drug testing for welfare benefits.[41] They previously recalled progressive school-board members and a lax-on-crime district attorney.[42] State Sen. Scott Wiener, D-San Francisco, even inserted special oversight powers of the city's permitting agency in a new state law that promotes housing construction.[43] This counterbalance was a long time in the making.

Governments are by their nature hard to reform, dominated as they are by the public-sector unions that represent the people who work for cities and by other special interests

Despite that encouraging news, San Francisco is still a far cry from operating in an efficient manner. The obvious problems are evident everywhere. The recent scandal about the city's long delays in building a $1.7 million public toilet at a park in the Noe Valley neighborhood (even after private companies donated the toilet unit and agreed to pay the installation workers) became a national story because it wasn't an aberration.[44] It highlighted something that San Franciscans routinely complain about. Governments are by their nature hard to reform, dominated as they are by the public-sector unions that represent the people who work for cities and by other special interests. Large city governments are among the hardest to change. There's a natural desire for visionaries to start from scratch. Building a few more subsidized apartments in existing cities won't shake up the status quo or accomplish anything beyond the margins.

The "15 Minute City" concept – whereby residents can access all the shops, parks and necessities within a 15-minute walk, bike ride or transit journey – has made some headway in existing areas.[45] I view it largely as an urbanist fad. It seems tailored mainly for relatively wealthy residents (young urban professionals, retirees or at-home tech workers) who don't have to, say, get to a roofing job or construction site or delivery destination farther out. But whatever its value, it's easier to implement in a newly designed city rather than an older one. I have nothing against the concept, by the way – more choices for more people is my mantra. But I'm not foolish enough to believe it to be a model for everyone, or something that's easy to retrofit.

> *Large city governments are among the hardest to change. There's a natural desire for visionaries to start from scratch.*

And let's not forget the degree to which urban dwellers are fleeing, something sparked by pandemic work-at-home expansions that relieved many workers from traditional commutes. Between 2018 and 2023, San Francisco lost nearly 9% of its population (although it's slowly started to grow again).[46] California cities dominate national lists of cities with declining populations. Los Angeles' population didn't fall so dramatically percentage-wise given its huge size, but its population has fallen to 2010 levels. One need not be conspiratorial to wonder whether some urbanist policies are designed more to prop up declining city tax bases and plummeting transit ridership rates rather than to improve the lives of the citizenry. That's where new cities and planned communities come into play and offer such an encouraging number of possibilities on various reform fronts.

America's Long History of Building New Cities

AS WE PONDER POTENTIAL new cities, it's worth looking at the nation's long history of building them. Instead of spending decades battling encrusted political systems in an effort to modestly reform their crime, housing and education policies, why not just start afresh and embrace sensible policies from the start? Again, new cities are nothing new. All cities were once vacant fields. Wealthy visionaries – including, as noted above, national heroes such as William Penn – have always lacked patience with encrusted bureaucracy and have been eager to try something new.

Here are some samples of new cities from the distant and not-so-distant past.

Orange County: Masters of master planning

Most people think of Orange County, the 3-million-plus population suburban county south of Los Angeles, as the heart and soul of national Republican politics. It's still considered Reagan country, even though the county has become urbanized, ethnically diverse and politically "purple." In a recent column, *The Washington Post's*

George Will noted that, "The region's single-family dwellings (few apartments) and car culture (negligible public transportation) produced a property-centered, aspirational, individualistic orientation of life with 'intensely middle-class values.'"[47]

One needn't be a Republican, however, to admire the way Orange County developers perfected the master-planning concept. Irvine is a stand-out example. The city now boasts a population of 314,000, making it the 13th-largest city in California. Unlike San Francisco, Irvine's population has grown around 12% since 2020. It topped the list as the nation's safest city based on its violent-crime statistics for 18 years in a row for cities in its size bracket.[48] It actually has an impressive skyline, is a major Southern California job center and is awash in shopping and other urban amenities. Much of the city is car dependent, of course, but it has plenty of walkability.

Writing for the urbanist website *Places Journal*, architect and historian Alan Hess toured developments in Irvine where he found typical houses along a greenbelt that were a short walk to the library, schools, recreation centers, shopping centers, offices and restaurants. He found extensive bike paths, parks and a wide mix of housing. It was far different than the typical sprawling suburbs that urbanists have long decried: "Here were all the progressive fundamentals taught at architecture and planning schools since the 1920s (earlier if you count Ebenezer Howard): superblocks, pedestrian paths, mixed uses, integrated landscaping, public amenities."[49] This was all by design.

The Irvine Ranch was originally acquired from a Spanish land grant and was home to ranching and agricultural pursuits. As metropolitan Los Angeles spread southward, the ranch's owners were reluctant to sell off their 185 square-mile property in a piecemeal fashion, per Hess. At the time, the University of California envisioned a new campus in the area. Architect William Pereira proposed a plan that would build "a new university-city, combined to amplify the advantages of both, founded on progressive planning principles and dedicated to modern architecture," Hess added.[50] "The plan's boldness appealed to Californians in the midst of a phenomenal expansion fueled by aerospace technology, television and cultural innovations in music, fashion, architecture and design." It was a new city built around the latest planning concepts and centered on a major university.

Irvine wasn't the only master-planned city built on Orange County ranchland, bean fields and orange groves. These include Rancho Mission Viejo, Coto de Caza, Rancho Santa Margarita, Ladera and Foothill Ranch. In fact, the private developments at the previously mentioned Great Park are master-planned communities that are among the fastest-growing in the nation.[51] All of these projects are essentially new cities, although because of their suburban character it's rare to find urbanists beyond Hess touting their benefits – even though they have generally epitomized the best practices in urban planning at the time of their inception. Some have gone on to become incorporated cities. These cities and neighborhoods are well known for their quality public services.

Reston, Va., and Columbia, Md.: An eastern take on the concept

Two of the most prominent new towns from the 1960s were built on the outskirts of Washington, D.C. They are somewhat closer to Washington (21 and 30 miles) than the proposed Solano city is to San Francisco, but the concept is the same – and at the time of their initial development they were placed on exurban and rural land. Both of these cities also embraced the concepts of walkability and greenbelts that echo what the New Urbanists promote today.

In his 1962 master plan for Reston, developer Robert E. Simon Jr. argued that, "The demands of the modern age require new concepts in the development of new communities. One of the principal goals for Reston is to build a balanced community, with facilities and social organization that can help meet the human requirements of our civilization."[52] Showing himself to be a visionary, Simon argued that, "Modern automated technology, with its shorter work day and shorter work week, brings with it a greater emphasis on the use of leisure." The goal was to integrate parks, golf courses, tennis courts, bike paths and other amenities to foster a better use of leisure time. The 15.7-square-mile area promised to have as many as 75,000 residents by 1980. Its population currently sits at 62,000, but it certainly has grown into a vibrant and sought-after Washington-area city.[53]

In 1967, developer James Rouse conceived the plan for Columbia. As an article published by the Federal Reserve Bank of Richmond explains, "Like Reston, Columbia was built on a vision of livability and integration. Its motto, 'The Next America,' was meant to capture Rouse's hope that the community could serve as an example of pragmatic utopianism for other communities across the nation – that is, an example of social interaction and harmony that, in Rouse's words, could provide 'an alternative to the mindlessness, the irrationality, the unnecessity of sprawl and clutter as a way of accommodating the growth of the American city.'"[54] Today, Columbia has a population of 107,000 people. It has a remarkably interesting downtown known for its arts venues and other amenities.

"Though the town hailed as 'the Next America' at its founding didn't quite hold to Rouse's original vision, experts say it has hung together remarkably well," concluded a 2017 retrospective in *The*

Baltimore Sun. "Even as urban design has evolved, Rouse's ideals are far from obsolete, and his work has paved the way for a new generation of planned communities."[55] Today's urbanists criticize the city as having become too suburban, but it nevertheless epitomized many of the principles they advocate today. I view the Solano proposed city as the latest iteration of this decades-old concept.

Foster City, Calif.: a small precursor to Solano?

Creating new cities from scratch isn't unheard of even in the San Francisco Bay Area. Although Foster City – on the San Francisco Peninsula abutting the San Mateo-Hayward Bridge – is a small community just 22 miles south of San Francisco, it often is compared conceptually to Columbia and Reston. Founded in 1958 in what was then a rural area known mainly for farming and salt producers along the San Francisco Bay, Foster City grew out of the same New Town movement. Its special twist was the incorporation of a system of lagoons that created a recreational nexus between the neighborhoods.

Writing for California Polytechnic University, planner Kalvin Platt explained the thinking behind this new community: "The plan encouraged a wide range of housing types, even in the early phases and a balanced relationship of living and working areas. It emphasized the development of distinctive types of housing for 'accommodation of the full life cycle for most of the population,' and 'a full component of community facilities (schools, parks, shopping centers, churches, etc.) for the resident population.' Also, the plan set processes for architectural review. Unique features in the neighborhood areas were 'micro-neighborhoods.' The larger neighborhood areas were broken into smaller units of 50 lots and approximately 200 people to which 'the resident can readily identify.'"[56]

It currently has 32,000 residents, which is on target with its original population goals. Platt argues that the city continues to offer lessons for modern urban planners in terms of neighborhood design, access to transit and myriad recreational amenities. Of course, Foster City no longer is a bastion of affordability, with a median home price of around $1.9 million.[57] That's not the fault of its planners, but of Bay Area housing problems caused by insufficient new construction. Had Bay Area governments permitted more such cities on the vast tracts of open, growth-protected land surrounding the metropolitan area, perhaps home prices wouldn't be as high as they are today.

Levittown, N.Y.: post-war suburban lessons

The concept of master-planned U.S. suburbs first sprung forth after World War II, when returning veterans were looking for homes in a world that had been quickly transformed by the automobile. As a *Los Angeles Times* article explained in 1988:

> The GIs were home from World War II, and housing was in short supply. Many veterans and their young families were forced to live with relatives, often in cramped city apartments. The suburbs? They were mostly for the rich and upper-middle class. But that year, a construction firm named Levitt & Sons, led by William J. Levitt changed suburbia forever. About 10 miles east of New York, on a potato field in Long Island, Levitt began building rows of relatively inexpensive two-bedroom houses at breakneck speed. Available only to World War

II veterans and their families – and only white veterans at that – the first Levittown house cost $6,990 with nearly no money down. Levitt built 17,447 houses in the next four years.[58]

Levitt replicated his idea in Bucks County, Pa., just north of Philadelphia. He also built communities in New Jersey and Puerto Rico. Modern planners often rightly critique Levittown because of its original discriminatory practices, which sadly reflected disturbing social restrictions at the time. They also criticize it for being the first mass-produced, car-dependent suburb. The original communities lacked commercial areas or downtowns or the kind of recreational amenities modern new cities feature. But the Levittown concept showed that developers can respond to vast housing shortages. These communities reflected the needs of the time. They've evolved over the years. Planners can learn from these early suburban developments and adjust their plans to modern ideas.

And Levittown critics often overlook the key point in the *Times* article:[59] The country was facing a vast housing shortage, with Americans crammed into apartments. Building new communities – even though we would build them differently today – provided opportunities for returning GIs to own decent homes with yards and start families. Levittown helped fuel the Baby Boom. In fact, I was raised in a similar suburb a few miles from Levittown, Pa.

Early utopian cities: nothing new under the sun

Urban thinkers have long tinkered with the form of our cities. In the United States, a wide variety of religious and utopian groups created new cities that conformed to their ideals. The History Channel reports that 80 such communities were formed in the 1840s.[60] These include Brook Farm in Massachusetts, the Oneida Community in New York, Shaker communities in Ohio and Kentucky, and Nauvoo in Illinois. The latter, built by adherents of the Latter Day Saints, boasted 30,000 residents at its prime, although now has a population of less than 1,000. Some of these communities had a cult-like feel to them, being conceived around concepts including free love, spiritualism, socialism or a strict adherence to religious doctrine.

None of these communities endured, with most of them now operating as fascinating tourist sites – not surprising given that they lacked widespread appeal. Nevertheless, these efforts to build new cities offer design lessons for modern planners and architects and echo some niche trends today. As a 2020 article in *Architectural Digest* explained, "The idea that community-focused movements are ways of enacting social change is just as relevant today as it was in the 19th century. Instead of attempting to create a perfect society through shared farm work, innovative architecture or time-saving devices, today's iterations focus on issues like climate change, food security and the benefits of intergenerational housing. At this point, it remains to be seen whether these modern utopian experiments will have more success than their predecessors, or if perfection will continue to remain frustratingly out of our reach."[61]

I suspect any projects designed around narrow interests or demanding some sort of perfection are ultimately designed to fail. But these early utopian experiments show that broad lifestyle visions often are dependent on the built environment. In the 19th century, advocates for, say, communal living built neighborhoods that facilitated their founders' ideals. These days, some developers have constructed car-free communities that conform to their goal of a walkable city free from car dependency. That's fine for those who want to live that way provided it's privately funded and voluntary. Modern advocates for such communities call them "intentional communities,"[62] referring to private developments and communities built around any number of shared interests or even embracing communal living. I can't imagine many living arrangements that would be more annoying for me, but to each their own.

Indeed, the market – if government allows it to operate properly – can respond to whatever potential buyers prefer, however broad or narrow. But while utopian concepts might have a niche place within the market, new cities obviously need to conform to the requirements of a wide population if they want to be more than a tourist curiosity 175 years from now.

Rethinking Ebenezer Howard's Garden City

Howard's name keeps popping up and for good reason. That's because modern planning concepts, including the ones discussed by California Forever, sometimes echo his thinking. In fact, his idea was for a private Garden City company to operate the cities independently of public agencies. He talked about sustainability and promoted the use of greenbelts, neighborhoods that accommodated a variety of socio-economic groups and an efficient transit system. Several Garden Cities were created in England and are functioning cities today. In the United States, Radburn, N.J., is perhaps the best-known Garden City, even though it's a neighborhood within a city. Greenbelt, Md., outside of Washington, D.C., is a Garden City built as part of Franklin Delano Roosevelt's Resettlement Program.[63]

In his 1898 book, *Garden Cities of To-Morrow*, Howard argued for the need to combine the best elements of country living with the best elements of urban living: "Human society and the beauty of nature are meant to be enjoyed together. The two magnets must be made one. As man and woman by their varied gifts and faculties supplement each other, so should town and country. The town is the symbol of society – of mutual help and friendly co-operation, of fatherhood, motherhood, brotherhood, sisterhood, of wide relations between man and man – of broad, expanding sympathies – of science, art, culture, religion. And the country! The country is the symbol of God's love and care for man. All that we are and all that we have comes from it."[64]

My point is that the new city concept is deeply embedded in our society and that new plans for new cities are not aberrations – but part of the long history of urban design and experimentation, of utopian dreams and of efforts to create communities that meet nuts-and-bolts needs. And, also, it's clear that many modern urbanist concepts – distinct neighborhoods, residents from a variety of income levels, easy walks to amenities and stores, parkland and easy transportation – are nothing new. The Solano city isn't as radical an idea as some people suggest.

Even un-zoned Houston is home to master-planned new cities

Master planning isn't with its detractors. It's not for everyone. Many people prefer the hurly burly of unplanned urban life. I generally find older communities, which have developed often in a haphazard and more natural manner to be more visually interesting than planned ones. These are just preferences. Both forms can – and should – coexist. One of the major problems with the urban-planning profession is its lack of diverse thought. It's rare to find an urban thinker who doesn't promote the New Urbanist agenda – and, more troubling, who doesn't believe that it is the only proper design for every community. The Congress for the New Urbanism, for instance, envisions a set of only six types of appropriate planning zones.[65]

Urbanists often disdain Houston, for instance, because of its lack of zoning. In their view, it has led to a sprawling, car-dependent city with a low density. I actually love Houston, aside from its hot and humid weather. Years ago, I heard one of its former mayors explain why the city, with its mostly market-based development patterns, has long been a bastion of opportunity for everyone. Here's what I wrote in a 2008 blog for *The Orange County Register*:

> Former Houston Mayor Bob Lanier, an old-school Democrat who ran the nation's fourth-largest city between 1992 and 1998, told those of us who attended the American Dream Coalition (ADC) conference in his city last week that he moved there from a poor, industrial city in East Texas because Houston was "an open city." A person's race or economic background didn't much matter even when he got there decades ago, and it still doesn't matter much in Houston today. Anyone who works hard, he said, can make it in Houston – a city that sophisticates decry as insufficiently planned (it still lacks zoning), too tacky (money is still what matters there) and too 'boom-to-bust.' Houston remains a place where fortunes soar and fall, and where brashness and bigness aren't frowned upon.[66]

That's why I promote markets. If government releases its grip, builders and developers and individual property owners and businesses can create the kind of urban environments that they choose. That provides the most opportunity and the best living conditions for everyone. Houston continues to enjoy rapid growth, with a metro population that now tops 7.3 million. In 2023, it was the second-fastest growing urban area in the country.[67] Because of its lack of growth controls, its median home price is a reasonable $340,000 compared to $1.2 million in the San Francisco Bay Area or $850,000 in metro Seattle. To the surprise of many observers, one needn't prefer the city of Houston's zoning-less ethos to enjoy living in the Houston area. The region has many master-planned communities that offer an alternative. The Woodlands, for instance, is a 28,500-acre planned community 31 miles from Houston. It has a population of 118,000 people.[68] In a functioning land-use market, buyers can pick and choose the type of community design that appeals to them. Median prices in The Woodlands are a relatively high $525,000, but still lower than most Western markets.

Ironically, Houston has gotten renewed positive attention from more open-minded urbanists. A 2013 article in *Governing* magazine noted the trend – which has become more pronounced in the following decade – toward higher-density, mixed-use projects. Because of its lack of zoning controls, developers have been able to respond to the increased demand for denser living. The writer, Ryan Honeywell, explains that "developers and city leaders who don't always see eye to eye generally believe the arrangement has worked in Houston's favor over the years, allowing developers to respond quickly to market conditions and keep housing costs low. Regardless of individual Houstonians' views on zoning, that part of the system is probably not changing. Four attempts at altering it have all failed. What is changing is Houstonians' attitude toward urban life."[69]

As more Houstonians embrace urbanist concepts, the market has provided more urbanist projects. Fancy that. Last year, urban planner William Fulton noted that urbanists have been wrong to ignore Houston as "a place capable of achieving practically anything. Houston's parks and bayou greenways are the envy of the country. The city's business leaders are leaning into the energy transition. And as cities rethink conventional zoning – not least because zoning ordinances had racist roots a century ago – Houston's regulation-light approach to real estate development is gaining national attention."[70] Perhaps someday urbanists will understand that such a "regulation-light" approach can best yield their design preferences and in a way that doesn't undermine others' preferences. And perhaps because of Houston's approach, the metro area offers plenty of master-planned alternatives.

As an aside, the great urban writer Jane Jacobs was no fan of Ebenezer Howard or central planning in general. In her book, *The Death and Life of Great American Cities*, she had this valid critique about Howard's Garden City concept:

> Ebenezer Howard's vision of the Garden City would seem almost feudal to us. He seems to have thought that members of the industrial working classes would stay neatly in their class, and even at the same job within their class; that agricultural workers would stay in agriculture; that businessmen (the enemy) would hardly exist as a significant force in his Utopia; and that planners could go about their good and lofty work, unhampered by rude nay-saying from the untrained. It was the very fluidity of the new 19th-century industrial and metropolitan society, with its profound shiftings of power, people and money that agitated Howard so deeply.[71]

Yet as much as I admire Jacobs, we needn't choose between suburbia or dense cities or master-planned new towns and cities. A nation this large and diverse can accommodate all such development choices. There are pluses and minuses for all of those alternatives, but as long as alternatives exist there really is no problem. And I love the idea of experimenting with new city and town concepts (as long as they are from scratch and privately created and not imposed on existing communities) as much as I love the idea of Houston's "open city" approach.

A fresh look at the suburbs

One final thought before I delve into some of the most fascinating new-city questions. I believe that urban planners need to take a fresh, open-minded view of the suburbs. Some of their critiques about car dependency, sprawl and a lack of walkable areas are valid, but they often seem infused with a disdain for these communities and for the people who live there. As one of our occasional Free Cities Center writers, Andrew Smith, explains: The suburbs have been reimagining the built environment for decades. I'll quote from one of his columns, "An ode to the suburb":

> While suburbs are often considered devoid of community, the opposite is true. Community bonds are often forged around churches and religious organizations, and because suburban communities by their nature tend to cater to families with children, the school becomes the epicenter of that community. In my community, we felt welcomed almost immediately by seeing neighbors on our daily walks around the neighborhood, but even more

so by those we attend church with and see every Sunday, and forge even greater bonds at the Friday night high school football and basketball games.[72]

Instead of insisting that suburbs are soulless and devoid of community and in need of total rejection, urbanists should focus on enhancing them with additional amenities and community oriented features that make them better. The latter has been taking place for years. It's the rare suburb these days, at least here in northern California, that doesn't have bike lanes, a network of parks, civic centers, downtown areas and walkable places. The suburb I live in has even won national awards for its modern planning concepts. It has an Old Town, a fully connected trail system, an aquatics center and bus system. I need (and want) a car, but today's suburbs – whether built from scratch or through adaptation – are a far cry from the original Levittown.

Some Thought Experiments with New Cities

IN DEVELOPING NATIONS, the idea of building new cities or business zones with reduced regulations has taken on a more urgent feel, largely because of the corruption and dysfunction that plague many governments in Central America, Africa and Asia. We've seen the emergence of hundreds of Special Economic Zones (SEZs),[73] which enable developers to create privately run business-oriented areas and some also with neighborhoods. It's a move to spur economic growth in countries where governmental reform is unrealistic or too long in the making. Sometimes the governments themselves recognize the problem and create the SEZs.

Writing for the Free Cities Center last year, Thibault Serlet, the director of research at a business intelligence firm that helps investors finance the creation of new SEZs, provided case studies of some of these projects including Pedra Branca in Brazil. Because it is run by investors and more accountable to its residents, the city of 40,000 has been able to solve many infrastructure problems that other Brazilian cities have been unable to address.[74]

"One of the biggest infrastructure problems in the region is water management," he wrote. "As of 2020, only 47.7% of households in Brazil have access to sewage; whereas 100% of homes in Pedro Branca have sewage. Sewage and water is entirely managed by the Pedra Branca Water and Sewage System."

Although developed nations such as the United States have largely conquered these problems, our country – and California in particular – has been struggling with basic governance issues that offer new opportunities for private zones or entire cities. Competition might help.

"Californians now face increasing government corruption, rising crime rates, lack of housing, hostile environments for business and long term poverty," Serlet notes. "The current state of urban decay is giving Americans their first taste of the challenges billions of people in emerging markets face on a daily basis."[75]

Private approaches offer a way to break the logjam. In his Free Cities Center booklet, *Latin America's Urban Experience*,[76] market urbanist writer Scott Beyer detailed how poor Latin American countries have turned to private providers to offer transit service and other necessities that typically are provided by the public sector. His booklet examines startup cities such as Prospera in Honduras, which has thrived (even as surrounding traditional cities have faltered) because of its low taxes, limited regulations, minimal zoning laws and private educational system.

Obviously, any American approach would need to reflect our nation's sensibilities and quality of life, but we can learn urban lessons from these SEZ models. This is where the Solano city idea is so enticing. Again, its proponents have not released many details about how it might be run, but I've argued that it can be a game-changer[77] if the developers embrace innovative approaches toward building infrastructure and running the nuts-and-bolts of city government.

It's hard to effect meaningful change in municipal governments. Even the best efforts often run aground. It can take years to change the political climate and the bureaucracy. I previously mentioned Sandy Springs, Ga., which in 2005 voted to incorporate as a city and contract out most services to a private firm. As the libertarian Reason Foundation explained shortly thereafter, "City leaders started with a blank slate, enabling them to ask fundamental questions about what role government should play. Every 'traditional' service or function was required to prove its worthiness and proper role and place within government, and officials had to decide whether to 'make' or 'buy' public services."[78] At the time, it was the sixth-largest city in Georgia and other cities followed suit.

This isn't that unusual of a model even in our country. Early in my career, I worked for an Air Force base that specialized in aeronautical testing that was run almost entirely by three separate outside contractors. The contracts came up every few years and were competitively bid. This process yielded cost savings and applied competitive pressure. If the contractor didn't handle things well or cost efficiently, it risked being replaced when the contract came up. Generally, government agencies contract out construction services.

Unfortunately, Sandy Springs has pulled back from this approach.[79] Citing decreased cost savings, in 2019 the city brought several of its outsourced departments back into the public fold. Nevertheless, the experiment provided a model for boosting competition. The more experimentation the better. I've reported on Anaheim, Calif.'s efforts in the mid-2000s to provide a "Freedom Friendly Anaheim" model that sought to reduce governmental burdens and make the city's planning department more customer friendly. A change in political leadership ultimately scuttled that plan, but urbanists ought to celebrate experimentation (through public or private changes) rather than relying on the usual immovable forces of government business as usual.[80]

The Solano project opened up many possibilities. Free Cities Center writer Edward Ring, in a two-part series last year, did some brainstorming about the project. He wondered about the aesthetics, the neighborhood design, the transportation network and its approach to providing public services and infrastructure. Ring pointed to the potential in terms of resource provision, energy production and waste recycling.[81] Plenty of innovative technologies exist to make the new city truly sustainable. Too often, "sustainability" is an environmentalist buzzword with no precise meaning, but a new city can actually produce all of its energy and recycle all of its waste. It's too bad we won't soon get to see how those issues would be resolved.

Brainstorming about new cities is fun. It tickles the imagination and for good reason. Blank slates provide an opportunity to rethink everything. But Ring also warns that envisioned utopians can easily descend into dystopias.[82] The website *ATI* (All That's Interesting) published a feature on 34 Chinese ghost cities, which are an example of central planning run amok: "Extravagant monuments, spacious parks, modern buildings, and interconnected roads would all seem to indicate a bustling metropolis. But in China, there is an increasing number of uninhabited 'ghost' cities that seem to have been abandoned after years of construction."[83] Such fears, however, are far more likely when an authoritarian government is dictating outcomes from its bureaus. There's far less risk of ensuing dystopia when private companies use their own money and limited authority to build new projects. I can't help but think about how poorly many of our current cities are run. I've currently been trying for two months to get someone in a city where I own a rental property to get back to me with an answer to a simple question about trimming a city owned tree. It's imperative that Americans try to find better ways to provide basic governance.

A group called the Free Cities Foundation (no relation to the Pacific Research Institute's Free Cities Center) supports the creation of startup cities across the globe. Unlike SEZs or Free Trade Zones, these autonomous cities are designed to create residential communities that provide "more freedom and a better life to full residential communities, rather than simply offering advantages to businesses."[84] The foundation exists precisely to answer these kinds of questions. For starters, the group proposes the creation of a Citizen Contract that details the benefits offered by these private cities, as well as the obligations of those who live there.

It notes that government is fundamentally a service: "So why not enter into a service contract with the government? In principle, government *is* a service like any other. You expect something from it – first and foremost the protection of life, liberty and property – and you are willing to pay in exchange. True, many expect a lot more from the state and don't want to pay for it. But they are OK if their freedom is therefore limited to large degrees. Insofar as reciprocity is generally accepted: if you want something, you have to give something in exchange."[85]

Why a contract when Americans, in particular, already live under the Constitution? The answer, from the foundation: "Constitutions can be changed, even against the will of the people concerned, provided there is a (qualified) majority. Contracts, on the other hand, only if the contracting party agrees. That is why the contract with each individual and the corresponding legal position are so important."[86] The foundation deals in practicalities (even as it raises some thought-provoking, boundary-pushing questions), but others promote new-city ideas that are filled with almost utopian promises and goals.

Axios reported in 2022 on a billionaire's plan to build a gee-whiz Jetsons-like city on 150,000 acres in the American desert.[87] Unlike the Solano city, this one touts futuristic architecture and a variety of far-reaching components: all vehicles would be electric or autonomous ones; all water would be stored, cleaned and reused on site; everything would be powered by renewables; and the entire city would be built around the 15-minute city concept. Called Telosa, its website is filled with gauzy, futuristic imagery – something that seems gleaned from a science-fiction movie.[88]

Its promises are far more grandiose than the practical ones championed by California Forever: "Imagine living in a city with an economic system in which citizens have a stake in the land; as the city does better, the residents do better." Telosa's supporters even coin a new term for their approach: "Equitism."[89] Some of these economic ideas harken back to Ebenezer Howard, who detailed an entire economic system to support his Garden Cities. *Axios* adds that there are a dozen proposals worldwide for utopian new cities.[90] Personally, I find the Solano idea (and the one touted by the Free Cities Foundation) more grounded in practicality and reality – and more likely to come to fruition provided government restrictions don't get in the way.

Conclusion: Let the Market Spur New Cities and Other Innovations

MY CRITIQUE WITH URBANISTS is that, in their desire to build better cities, they lack confidence in the marketplace, which is nothing more than the embodiment of the decentralized ideas of a free people making their own decisions and investments. Urbanists often tout deregulation, but only in limited ways that result in their desired outcomes. Yet when market forces are unleashed, we find innovation, reform and new ideas. We might like some of the results and dislike others, but not every human being likes the same thing. But nothing great comes from too much government control, which stifles change and improvement. Or as Jane Jacobs once complained, "As in all utopias, the right to have plans of any significance belonged only to the planners in charge."[91] The key – in new cities or old ones – is to let individuals chart their own future, rather than make them dependent on government planners.

In a March 2024 column in the conservative *National Review* called "Make Communities Friendly Again," writer Patrick T. Brown pointed to the regulatory barriers that local governments impose on those who want to build new projects: "Cities and suburbs can overregulate in a way that makes it difficult to experiment with a less rigid, more organic style of living."[92] Indeed. The answer isn't a new one-size-fits-all regimen of urbanist regulation, but deregulation – and most important in the context of this booklet, allowing developers to experiment with new concepts on open land. Such experimentation can unleash unforeseen innovations that improve urban life.

Endnotes

1   Ben Christopher, "Year in review: California homelessness worsens even as housing bills pass," *CalMatters*, Dec. 19, 2023, https://calmatters.org/housing/2023/12/california-homelessness-housing/

2   Steven Greenhut, "Sorry, urbanists, but bicycles will never save the planet," *Orange County Register*, Nov. 10, 2023, https://www.ocregister.com/2023/11/10/sorry-urbanists-but-bicycles-will-never-save-the-planet/

3   Staff, "Video: Why Housing Policy is Climate Policy," California YIMBY, Oct. 13, 2021, https://cayimby.org/blog/video-why-housing-policy-is-climate-policy/

4   Editorial Board, "Surf City goes all in to push NIMBY agenda," *Orange County Register*, March 1, 2023, https://www.ocregister.com/2023/03/01/surf-city-goes-all-in-to-push-nimby-agenda/

5   Wendell Cox, "Planners push transit, but it's a hard sell in Western cities," Free Cities Center, Nov. 10, 2022, https://www.pacificresearch.org/planners-push-transit-but-its-a-hard-sell-in-western-cities/

6   Katie Dowd, "First map of proposed utopian California city in Solano County is released," *San Francisco Chronicle*, Jan. 17, 2024, https://www.sfgate.com/bayarea/article/map-utopi-an-california-city-solano-county-18612996.php

7   Nick McConnell, "California Forever removes initiative from November ballot," *Vacaville Reporter*, July 22. 2024, https://www.thereporter.com/2024/07/22/california-forever-re-moves-initiative-from-november-ballot/

8   "The orderly growth idea," Solano County Orderly Growth Committee, accessed April 14, 2024, https://solanoorder-lygrowth.org/the-idea

9   Initiative language, "East Solano Homes, Jobs and Clean Energy Initiative," accessed April 14, 2024, https://downloads.ctfassets.net/ivxuf0dn6dhw/6p3T8ccrYuqrvj7BBO7khw/fba3cf4d7ca54dfdc4054e3717d7bf70/2024-02-14_Initiative.pdf

10   Conor Daugherty and Erin Griffith, "The Silicon Valley Elite Who Want to Build a City From Scratch," *New York Times*, Aug. 25, 2023, https://www.nytimes.com/2023/08/25/busi-ness/land-purchases-solano-county.html

11   Cassie Armstrong, "Disney World at 50: Fake companies and secret deals acquired land for Magic Kingdom," *Orlando Sentinel*, April 7, 2021, https://www.orlandosentinel.com/2021/04/07/disney-world-at-50-fake-companies-and-se-cret-deals-acquired-land-for-magic-kingdom/#:~:text=In%201964%2C%20Walt%20Disney%20used,suspicion%2C%20wh-ile%20keeping%20prices%20low.

12   Conor Daugherty and Erin Griffith, "The Silicon Valley Elite Who Want to Build a City From Scratch," *New York Times*, Aug. 25, 2023, https://www.nytimes.com/2023/08/25/busi-ness/land-purchases-solano-county.html

13   California Forever website, accessed April 14, 2024, https://
     californiaforever.com/?gad_source=1&gclid=CjwKCAjw_
     e2wBhAEEiwAyFFFoz-Y-sRSeUzJlZX70bwLLqIsgsqSOD-
     PuTuVotmhKjUgq3gpNPmxoVxoCdzYQAvD_BwE

14   Ibid.

15   Ibid.

16   Editorial Board, "Great Park hungry for pork," *Orange
     County Register*, March 29, 2009, https://www.ocregister.
     com/2009/03/29/editorial-great-park-hungry-for-pork/

17   Alan Ehrenhalt, "A Possible Future for Downtowns Out in
     the Suburbs," *Governing*, Spring 2024, https://www.gov-
     erning.com/urban/a-possible-future-for-downtowns-out-
     in-the-suburbs

18   Krys Shahin, "California Forever lawsuit against farmers to
     continue in court, judge rules," ABC10 News, April 2, 2024,
     https://www.abc10.com/article/news/local/vacaville/califor-
     nia-forever-lawsuit-judge-rules/103-faf6f296-c18d-47f5-
     9f6f-bbcd9e856052

19   Jonathan Ayestas, "Billionaire group proposing new city in
     Solano County remakes map after air base's flight concerns,"
     KCRA, Feb. 16, 2024, https://www.kcra.com/article/califor-
     nia-forever-new-city-map-travis-air-force-base/46823479

20   Ashley Sharp, "California Forever accused of deceitfully gath-
     ering signatures in push to get measure on November ballot,"
     CBS News, March 22, 2024, https://www.cbsnews.com/sac-
     ramento/news/california-forever-accused-deceitfully-gather-
     ing-signatures-november-ballot-measure/

21   Statement, "Flannery's Proposed New Town," Sierra Club
     Redwood Chapter, accessed April 14, 2024, https://www.
     sierraclub.org/redwood/flannery-s-proposed-new-town

22 Adhiti Bandlamudi, "California Forever Faces Resistance From Federal Lawmakers and Local Leaders in Solano County," KQED, Feb. 16, 2024, https://www.kqed.org/news/11976108/california-forever-faces-resistance-from-federal-lawmakers-and-local-leaders-in-solano-county

23 Shira Stein, "California Forever developers could create their own de facto government, lawmakers warn," *San Francisco Chronicle*, Feb. 15, 2024, https://www.sfchronicle.com/politics/article/california-forever-government-18665568.php

24 David Segal, "A Georgia Town Takes the People's Business Private," *New York Times*, June 23, 2012, https://www.nytimes.com/2012/06/24/business/a-georgia-town-takes-the-peoples-business-private.html

25 Solano County website, Review of county report of East Solano Plan, https://www.solanocounty.com/news/displaynews.asp?NewsID=2533&TargetID=1, accessed July 27, 2024

26 Steven Greenhut interviews Nick McConnell and Edward Ring, "Learn about the intriguing proposed Solano County city," Free Cities Center video, March 13, 2024, https://www.pacificresearch.org/watch-learn-about-the-intriguing-proposed-solano-county-city/

27 Ibid.

28 John Seiler, "'Urban growth boundaries' make cities less affordable," Free Cities Center, Dec. 2, 2022, https://www.pacificresearch.org/urban-growth-boundaries-make-cities-less-affordable/

29 Steven Greenhut and Wayne Winegarden, "Giving Housing Supply a Boost," Free Cities Center, January 2024, https://www.pacificresearch.org/urban-growth-boundaries-make-cities-less-affordable/

30 Statement, "Smart Growth Principles," *Smart Growth Online*, accessed April 14, 2024, https://smartgrowth.org/smart-growth-principles/

31 Video, "Tour a public-private partnership that is transforming Sacramento," Free Cities Center, Aug. 14, 2023, https://www.pacificresearch.org/tour-a-public-private-partnership-that-is-transforming-sacramento/

32 California YIMBY, "Statement in Support of East Solano Plan," June 24, 2024, https://cayimby.org/news-events/statement-in-support-of-the-east-solano-plan/

33 Josie Huang, "Searching for Solutions to SoCal's Housing Crisis, YIMBYs Say 'Yes' to Development," KQED, Sept. 1, 2017, https://www.kqed.org/news/11615303/searching-for-solutions-to-socals-housing-crisis-yimbys-say-yes-to-development

34 Devin Trubey, "Solano Coalition opposing new city California Forever launches," ABC 10, Feb. 4, 2024, https://www.abc10.com/article/news/local/solano-coalition-opposing-california-forever-launches/103-6b1aaf08-bdf0-4e52-bc8e-fbef48a0a939

35 J.K. Dineen, "An urban dream or Sprawl 2.0," *San Francisco Chronicle*, Sept. 9, 2023, https://www.sfchronicle.com/bayarea/article/solano-county-new-city-18351062.php

36 Ibid.

37 Solano Together website, accessed April 14, 2024, https://www.solanotogether.org/about

38 Ibid.

39   Heather Knight and Shawn Hubler, "San Francisco's Woes Are Well Known. Across the Bay, Oakland Has Struggled More," *New York Times*, Dec. 14, 2022, https://www.ny-times.com/2023/12/14/us/oakland-crime-economy-home-lessness.html

40   Derek Thompson, "The Future of the City is Childless," *The Atlantic*, July 18, 2019, https://www.theatlantic.com/ideas/archive/2019/07/where-have-all-the-children-gone/594133/

41   Reis Thebault, "San Francisco, the liberal beacon, embraces conservative ballot measures," *Washington Post*, March 7, 2024, https://www.washingtonpost.com/nation/2024/03/07/san-francisco-welfare-drug-screening-police/

42   Sam Levin, "San Francisco recalls DA Chesa Boudin in blow to criminal justice reform," *The Guardian*, June 7, 2022, https://www.theguardian.com/us-news/2022/jun/07/san-francis-co-vote-chesa-boudin-recall

43   Annie Gaus, "San Francisco housing crisis: New state bill may force city to build faster," *San Francisco Standard*, Sept. 15, 2023, https://sfstandard.com/2023/09/15/san-francisco-sin-gled-out-in-state-housing-bill-that-speeds-up-development/

44   Heather Knight, "S.F. Toiletgate: City is being gifted a free bathroom, but it's still going to cost $1 million," *San Francisco Chronicle*, Jan. 21, 2023, https://www.sfchronicle.com/sf/bayarea/heatherknight/article/noe-valley-town-square-17731989.php

45   Michael J. Coren, "How the suburbs could become 15-minute cities," *Washington Post*, Nov. 28, 2023 https://www.washing-tonpost.com/climate-environment/2023/11/28/15-minute-ci-ty/

46   Jaclyn DeJohn, "Here's where San Francisco ranks in terms of population loss in the past 5 years," KRON, Dec. 1, 2023, https://www.kron4.com/news/bay-area/heres-where-san-francisco-ranks-in-terms-of-population-loss-in-the-past-5-years/

47   George Will, "Republicans aim to regain what used to be their California stronghold," *Washington Post*, Aug. 16, 2023, https://www.washingtonpost.com/opinions/2023/08/16/orange-county-republican-hopes/

48   Statement, Irvine Safest City for 18th Year, city of Irvine, accessed April 14, 2024, https://www.cityofirvine.org/news-media/news-article/irvine-safest-city-18th-year-0#:~:text=Irvine%20is%20the%20safest%20city%20of%20its%20size%20for%20violent,population%20of%20250%2C000%20or%20more.

49   Alan Hess, "Discovering Irvine," *Places Journal*, October 2014, https://placesjournal.org/article/discovering-irvine/

50   Ibid.

51   Jonathan Lansner, "3 Southern California communities among fastest-selling home projects in US," *Orange County Register*, Jan. 12, 2024, https://www.ocregister.com/2024/01/12/3-southern-california-communities-among-fastest-selling-home-projects-in-us/#:~:text=Southern%20California%20is%20home%20to,year%20%E2%80%93%20up%2070%25%20vs.

52   Robert E. Simon, "Reston Master Plan Report," March 10, 1963, https://reston50.gmu.edu/items/show/8

53   Ibid.

54 Emily Corcoran, "The Making of Reston and Columbia," *Econ Focus*, Federal Reserve Bank of Richmond, Second/Third Quarter 2020, https://www.richmondfed.org/publications/research/econ_focus/2020/q2-3/economic_history#:~:text=Fifty%20miles%20northeast%2C%20Columbia%2C%20Md,vision%20of%20livability%20and%20integration.

55 Doug Miller, "Planned cities have gone out of style, but Columbia still influences urban design," *Baltimore Sun*, June 8, 2017, https://www.baltimoresun.com/2017/06/08/planned-cities-have-gone-out-of-style-but-columbia-still-influences-urban-design/

56 Kalvin Platt, "Foster City – A New City on the Bay: A Tribute to Professor Michael McDougall," *Focus*, Cal Poly San Luis Obispo, Issue 1, 2008, https://digitalcommons.calpoly.edu/focus/vol5/iss1/8/

57 Foster City, California, Realtor.com, accessed April 14, 2024, https://www.realtor.com/realestateandhomes-search/Foster-City_CA/overview

58 James F. Peltz, "It Started With Levittown in 1947 : Nation's 1st Planned Community Transformed Suburbia," *Los Angeles Times*, June 21, 1988, https://www.latimes.com/archives/la-xpm-1988-06-21-fi-4744-story.html

59 Ibid.

60 Elizabeth Dunn, "5 19th-Century Utopian Communities in the United States," History Channel, Sept. 19, 2023, https://www.history.com/news/5-19th-century-utopian-communities-in-the-united-states

61 Elizabeth Yuko, "These Forward-Thinking Utopias Changed Design Forever," *Architectural Digest*, Aug. 4, 2020, https://www.architecturaldigest.com/story/utopian-communities-the-future

62 Cynthia Tina, "Intentional Communities: Beginners Guide to Life in Cooperative Culture," Community Finder, Dec. 16, 2022, https://communityfinders.com/intentional-communities/

63 Cassandra O'Donnell, "Garden Cities Around the World," *Urban Utopias*, Nov. 15, 2018, https://urbanutopias.net/2018/11/15/garden-cities-around-the-world/

64 Ebenezer Howard, *Garden Cities of To-Morrow*, 1902, Swan Sonnenschein & Co., https://centerforneweconomics.org/envision/library/general-collection/book-reports/garden-cities-of-tomorrow/

65 Congress for the New Urbanism, Tools, accessed April 14, 2024, https://www.cnu.org/resources/tools#:~:text=The%20rural%2Dto%2Durban%20Transect,do%20not%20fit%20into%20neighborhoods.

66 Steven Greenhut, "Closed case for 'open' cities," *Orange County Register*, May 25, 2008, https://www.ocregister.com/2008/05/25/closed-case-for-open-cities/

67 Yilun Cheng," Houston is second fastest-growing metro in U.S.," *Houston Chronicle*, April 12, 2023, https://www.houstonchronicle.com/news/houston-texas/article/houston-second-fastest-growing-metro-us-census-17888963.php

68 The Woodlands, Niche, accessed April 14, 2024, https://www.niche.com/places-to-live/the-woodlands-montgomery-tx/

69   Ryan Honeywell, "Houston: The Surprising Contender in America's Urban Revival," *Governing*, Sept. 25, 2013, https://www.governing.com/archive/gov-houston-urban-revival.html

70   William Fulton, "Urbanists used to ignore Houston. We were wrong.," *Houston Chronicle*, May 20, 2023, https://www.houstonchronicle.com/opinion/outlook/article/houston-urban-city-planning-rice-kinder-institiute-18107177.php

71   Jane Jacobs, "The Death and Life of Great American Cities," 1961, Random House, https://en.wikipedia.org/wiki/The_Death_and_Life_of_Great_American_Cities

72   Andrew Smith, "Ode to the suburb," Free Cities Center, Jan. 4, 2024, https://www.pacificresearch.org/?s=Ode+to+the+suburb

73   Special economic zones, Britannica Money, accessed April 14, 2024, https://www.britannica.com/money/special-economic-zone

74   Thibault Serlet, "Why do politicians hate planned communities?" Free Cities Center, Aug. 9, 2023, https://www.pacificresearch.org/why-do-politicians-hate-planned-communities/

75   Ibid.

76   Scott Beyer, *Latin America's Urban Experience,* Free Cities Center, October 2023, https://www.pacificresearch.org/latin-americas-experience-shows-how-markets-can-help-urban-america-overcome-government-created-problems/

77   Steven Greenhut, "Private city east of the Bay Area can be a game-changer," Free Cities Center, Sept. 9, 2023, https://www.pacificresearch.org/private-city-east-of-bay-area-could-be-a-game-changer/

78　Steve Stanek and Leonard Gilroy, "Sandy Springs Incorporates, Inspires New Wave of 'Private' Cities in Georgia," Reason Foundation, Nov. 1, 2006, https://reason.org/commentary/sandy-springs-incorporates-ins/

79　Arielle Cass and Ben Brasch, "Sandy Springs, first in cityhood, changes how it does business," *Atlanta Journal-Constitution*, May 17, 2019, https://www.ajc.com/news/local/sandy-springs-first-cityhood-changes-how-does-business/cRX2YPFD-VzWgUtNE7c4h9L/

80　Matthew Fleming, "How a freedom-friendly city descended into chaos," Free Cities Center, Sept. 9, 2022, https://www.pacificresearch.org/how-a-freedom-friendly-city-descended-into-chaos/

81　Edward Ring, "How a new city can change how California envisions its future: Part One," Free Cities Center, Sept. 22, 2023, https://www.pacificresearch.org/how-new-city-can-change-how-california-envisions-its-future-part-one/

82　Edward Ring, "How a new city can change how California envisions its future: Part Two," Free Cities Center, Sept. 29, 2023, https://www.pacificresearch.org/how-new-city-can-change-how-california-envisions-its-future-part-one-2/

83　Natasha Ishak, "34 Unforgettable Photos Of China's Uninhabited Ghost Cities," *ATI*, March 18, 2024, https://allthatsinteresting.com/chinese-ghost-cities

84　Free Cities Foundation, accessed April 14, 2024, https://free-cities.org/

85　Ibid.

86　Ibid.

87   Jennifer A. Kingson, "'Cities of the future,' built from scratch," *Axios*, https://www.axios.com/2022/08/25/city-of-the-future-neom-telosa-lore-mbs

88   Telosa website, accessed April 14, 2024, https://cityoftelosa.com/

89   Ibid.

90   Jennifer A. Kingson, "'Cities of the future,' built from scratch," *Axios*, https://www.axios.com/2022/08/25/city-of-the-future-neom-telosa-lore-mbs

91   Jane Jacobs, "The Death and Life of Great American Cities," 1961, Random House, https://en.wikipedia.org/wiki/The_Death_and_Life_of_Great_American_Cities

92   Patrick T. Brown, "Make Communities Friendly Again," *National Review*, March 31, 2024, https://www.nationalreview.com/2024/03/make-communities-friendly-again/

About the Author

STEVEN GREENHUT is a longtime journalist who has covered California politics since 1998. He wrote this book for the San Francisco-based Pacific Research Institute, where he founded that think tank's Sacramento-based journalism center in 2009. He currently is western region director for the R Street Institute, a Washington, D.C.-based free-market think tank, and is on the editorial board of the Southern California News Group. Greenhut has worked fulltime as a columnist for the *Orange County Register* and the *San Diego Union-Tribune*. He writes weekly for *American Spectator* and *Reason* magazines. He is the editor of *Saving California*, and the author of *Winning the Water Wars, Abuse of Power* and *Plunder.* He is also the author of the Free Cities Center booklets *Back from Dystopia: A New Vision for Western Cities, Putting Customers First: Re-Envisioning our Approach to Transportation Planning,* and *Giving Housing Supply a Boost: How to Improve Affordability and Reduce Homelessness* (with Dr. Wayne Winegarden).

About Pacific Research Institute

The Pacific Research Institute (PRI) champions freedom, opportunity, and personal responsibility by advancing free-market policy solutions. It provides practical solutions for the policy issues that impact the daily lives of all Americans, and demonstrates why the free market is more effective than the government at providing the important results we all seek: good schools, quality health care, a clean environment, and a robust economy.

Founded in 1979 and based in San Francisco, PRI is a non-profit, non-partisan organization supported by private contributions. Its activities include publications, public events, media commentary, community leadership, legislative testimony, and academic outreach.

Center for Business and Economics

PRI shows how the entrepreneurial spirit—the engine of economic growth and opportunity—is stifled by onerous taxes, regulations, and lawsuits. It advances policy reforms that promote a robust economy, consumer choice, and innovation.

Center for Education

PRI works to restore to all parents the basic right to choose the best educational opportunities for their children. Through research and grassroots outreach, PRI promotes parental choice in education, high academic standards, teacher quality, charter schools, and school-finance reform.

Center for the Environment

PRI reveals the dramatic and long-term trend toward a cleaner, healthier environment. It also examines and promotes the essential ingredients for abundant resources and environmental quality: property rights, markets, local action, and private initiative.

Center for Health Care

PRI demonstrates why a single-payer Canadian model would be detrimental to the health care of all Americans. It proposes market-based reforms that would improve affordability, access, quality, and consumer choice.

Center for California Reform

The Center for California Reform seeks to reinvigorate California's entrepreneurial self-reliant traditions. It champions solutions in education, business, and the environment that work to advance prosperity and opportunity for all the state's residents.

Center for Medical Economics and Innovation

The Center for Medical Economics and Innovation aims to educate policymakers, regulators, health care professionals, the media, and the public on the critical role that new technologies play in improving health and accelerating economic growth.

Free Cities Center

The Free Cities Center cultivates innovative ideas to improve our cities and urban life based around freedom and property rights – not government.

www.ingramcontent.com/pod-product-compliance
Lightning Source LLC
Chambersburg PA
CBHW070030030426
42335CB00017B/2373